THE 10 POWERFUL LESSONS
THAT MADE ME
A MILLIONAIRE

Think Rich, Grow Rich

Table of Content

Introduction:

Starting a financial mastery journey is an intense undertaking that has the power to completely transform your life. Motivated by a desire for financial plenty, I have read over 350 self-improvement books in my ceaseless quest for success. My initial driving force was a single goal: to make $10,000 each month. I had no idea that this adventure would not only improve my financial situation but also teach me priceless lessons that would change my life.

The financial counsel that I impart in this book, "The 10 powerful Lessons That Made Me a Millionaire," goes beyond the typical guidelines. Every lesson serves as a beacon to help you navigate the complex terrain of financial competence.

Chapter 1. Don't Live Below Your Means Expand Your Means

Don't Live Below Your Means Expand Your Means. I think this advice, came from Second Chance by Robert Kiyosaki. According to Kiyosaki, a financial planner will advise you to reduce your spending and save money. So you won't be purchasing the things you like, like dinner at your preferred restaurant.

Why don't we consider the other side of the equation, he asks?

Why don't we figure out how to make more money so that the cost of supper doesn't matter?

Spending less money kills passion. No one gets enthusiastic in the morning and decides to make a few small cost cuts here and there, in order for me to have some extra money.

Reducing expenses isn't inspiring. Always aim to increase your income rather than saying, "I can't afford it" say, how can I afford it?

I found that this advice made a lot of sense right away for two key reasons.

One, I came to see there was a limit to cost-cutting. You can really save money on a finite number of costs.

Two, I came to understand that my time and energy are what really matter. I can cut, say, $10 in an hour, or I can utilize the same energy to earn $100. I know individuals who maintain an Excel spreadsheet in which they list every item they purchase during the day.

Always look for ways to minimize costs; visit several stores to get a few bucks off. They use their meager resolve to prevent themselves from purchasing $5 items they adore. Since all of these demand a lot of energy, investing that effort into increasing your income seems like it will yield a higher return.

More money isn't all that frightening. To earn more is simply to solve more puzzles (problems). You get paid more, the more problems you solve. This is how the road to financial success and problem-solving looks. You begin by tackling little issues. Most of the time, these are personal issues like ignorance of certain subjects, or a deficiency in self-assurance. You then go on to ones that are more intricate. You advance to a new level where there is a new problem after you solve the previous one.

You become smarter and make more money the more financial problems you solve. It also has the opposite effect. You become impoverished the more financial issues you ignore.

Chapter 2."What's the Worst That Can Happen?" is a powerful tool for overcoming financial fear.

This lesson is taken from a personal development book called How to develop yourself, not a finance book. Dale Carnegie, "To Stop Worrying and Start Living." Still,

I've found it to be very helpful for business in general and investing in particular.

As you have undoubtedly observed, financial concerns account for the majority of our anxieties and tensions. What happens, for instance, if I invest in this business idea and it fails? What if I put all of my money into this company and lose it all? How can I repay a loan that I can't repay?

Before making a financial decision, whenever I experienced anxiety or fear, I would always ask myself this question: what is the worst that can happen if I do this? Carnegie argues that things we think are terrible are actually not as bad as we think. I wholeheartedly concur with this viewpoint and have personally seen it numerous times.

This inquiry instantly soothes you and makes it clear that even the worst case is not as awful as you believe. Frequently, you come to the realization that, in the worst situation, you could easily adjust to it.

Here's how you can use this in your personal situation.

First, honestly assess the circumstances and determine the worst case scenario.

Step two is to accept the worst case scenario after determining what it might be.

Accept it as it has already happened.

Step three: Calmly dedicate your time and energy to working after you've accepted the worst-case scenario on the issue.

Embracing the reality of the situation is the first step towards recovering from any bad luck. Worrying ruins our ability to focus, which is one of its worst effects. When we worry, our thoughts wander, but acceptance helps us to relax and concentrate on the resolution.

Chapter 3: The Wrong Mountain and The Sunk Cost Fallacy

Envision yourself ascending a mountain, and halfway there, you glance around and realize you've ascended the incorrect mountain. You made a mistake, and the mountain you had to climb is right next to you. To get on the right mountain, you must first descend, take a little break, make some plans, and then begin once more.

What do you do now? You are not going down if you're anything like most people. You're going to think, what the hell? Even though you know that's the right thing to do. Being on the wrong mountain stinks, but I'm not going down.

I can't throw away all of my hard work because I have worked so hard to get this far. In addition, I'm going to stay because the view isn't too bad. The majority of us have psychological barriers that prevent us from going down the wrong mountain known as the "sunk cost fallacy" It's the propensity to place a higher value on the energy or money we've already spent and fail to consider the money or energy we'll lose later.

Stated differently, we continue to prioritize the past over the future. Perhaps you are reading this book right now and thinking, "I would if I were on that mountain." descend and begin once more. Well, let me ask you this.

You followed your parents' wishes and became a doctor, engineer, or lawyer. By now, half of your studies are completed, and you already realize that this is the wrong mountain.

However, you persist in moving forward. For what reason is that the case? Even though you detest your job, you continue to do it and most likely will continue to do so for the remainder of your life. For what reason is that the case?

Even though you know a relationship with this person is not going to work, you continue to moving. You give up smoking and swear never to smoke again. You're hiding the last package somewhere in your room, rather than throwing it away.

I assume you already see my point.

One of the most prevalent and harmful cognitive biases to which humans are susceptible is the sunk cost fallacy. My life has greatly improved since I realized this. Though it's difficult, I try not to think about the money I've lost or the time and effort I've invested.

I remind myself that the past is the past and have spent. Furthermore, it is unimportant in terms of something's potential success in the future. Beginning today, knowing what I know now, I ask myself this question: what further putting money into this venture or connection.

Does it make sense to follow through on this choice as of right now, or not? I cease if the response is negative. To be honest, stopping hurt every single time. Although it hurt to waste all that effort and money, it was ultimately worthwhile.

For instance, I spent one and half semester at the university working on a diploma thesis, and finished more than 45 percent of the work before realizing I was in the wrong place.

I continued my education, destroyed all of my previous work, and began afresh. Looking back, it was unquestionably worthwhile. You wouldn't be reading this book right now if I hadn't done it because of my new diploma. My thesis focused on digital marketing and product management; I have worked with numerous businesses worldwide and have managed thousands of successful products.

It was a business case type of thesis where I researched how to manage and build strategic marketing pattern for different product from scratch and turn it into a consistent conversation path.

I enjoyed every minute of work I put into that thesis because I knew that I would implement it in real life.

I got a D as a final grade for my thesis, but I felt like I got an A. Please don't get me wrong, I'm not trying to brag or anything, I only tried to give you a real life example, and show you the beautiful things that can happen if you ignore the cost you have incurred, and decide to climb a new mountain.

Chapter 4. The Wealth Blueprint - Interpreting Assets and Debts

Rich Dad Poor Dad was one of the first few finance books I read, as is the case with many new readers. The distinction between an asset and a liability is the most significant lesson I have retained. Something that puts money in your pocket is an asset, according to Rich Dad, and a liability as something that depletes your financial resources.

Although very basic, this lesson is difficult to implement in everyday life.

Rich Dad said that all it takes to become wealthy is one simple thing to do. Purchase additional goods that will make you wealthy. I became aware of every purchase I was making after reading the book, and centered on acquiring additional assets. That concludes it.

One of the assets I purchased was a piece of real estate that was earning about $40 per day, with a positive cash flow.

Even though I was new to marketing at the time, I had already completed a few projects successfully and was making funds obtained from the projects. When I checked my earnings one day, I noticed that one of the projects had been generating about forty dollars a month on average.

For me, this was a wake-up call because it showed me the value of each and every campaign I completed for my classes. Every month, this digital real estate generates positive cash flow. Each month, the real estate asset and that project brought in an average of forty dollars.

However, it took me several months to buy the property, and it only cost me $12,000 in total. Even though I was only making a few hundred dollars a year working and marketing my courses, I loved every second of it.

I began to treat every project as a serious endeavor and to take marketing seriously at this point. Naturally, this resulted in the creation of an increasing number of courses covering an increasing number of topics.

Chapter 5: Relying Solely On Willpower Is Foolish When It Comes To Money

Instead, automate. I was having a meeting to get a credit card from my manager at the bank a few years ago. If you use a credit card, you are likely aware of how high interest rates can be. Credit card usage is high.

There is no interest if you repay the loan within the allotted time, but if you miss the free period, you'll have to pay a hefty interest rate.

Thus, I received a warning from my manager saying, "Look, you have two options to pay back the cash. First, and least expensively, you can simply create a calendar alert for the precise day of each month and make the payment by hand. To move the money, you just need to push one button. You don't even need to enter the account number because it's that simple. Simply designate a button on your calendar and push it once.

Alternatively, you can select a date and have the money taken out automatically. But each month, this automated system will set you back about $3. He said, "In my view, the first option is the best one." It is also very simple to do and free of cost. Paying for it makes no sense. Simply click to create a reminder on your calendar for the same day each month in your mobile app, a single button.

I followed his advice, thinking that it wouldn't be necessary to pay $3 a month when I am able to do it for free. You can probably guess what happened next. Over the next six months, I paid interest twice because I neglected to click that one little button.

For $50 the first time, and $60 the second. I easily could have paid for it and received a calendar reminder, but I still forgot to do it.

For instance, I once told myself that I would finish the notification later even though I was in the middle of something crucial at the time. And that time never arrived. I sent the guy an email after the second interest payment, requesting that he turn it on automatically.

He cautioned me about the $3 fee once more, but I had already learned my lesson. When it comes to managing your finances, investing, saving for a trip, or making payments, It won't happen if you don't set it up to happen automatically, be it debt or anything else.

You can still fail, regardless of how disciplined or strong your will is. I've always remembered this lesson, so I now try my best to let things happen on autopilot, not only in terms of money but in other domains as well. Because I am aware that using willpower alone will never be effective.

Psychology and emotions probably account for more than 90% of the work when it comes to money. The majority of the psychological and emotional resistance is eliminated by automation, which is its beautiful quality. After setting it once, you forget about it.

Chapter 6: The Invisible Cost of Ambition - Exposing the Price of Getting Richer

All things have a cost, but not all costs are indicated on labels. Now, I recognize that your goals are to become wealthy, independent, and successful business one day, and that's totally fine too.

However, wanting all of these and acting on them without thinking things through the cost that you must incur is not acceptable.

This is what I mean. Suppose I approached you and asked if you wanted to compete in mixed martial arts professionally, within the UFC.

You would undoubtedly believe that possessing the same fighting prowess as those guys would be incredible. But after thinking about it, I'm pretty sure you're going to turn down my offer.

The reason is that you know it will take an incredible amount of effort, time, and most likely a few severe injuries, to reach average. Not to mention pursue a career in it.

You wouldn't accept it since you don't want to work out for five or six hours every day, occasionally even twice a day. You don't want to spend the majority of your life on a diet and consuming bland food.

Arguments about you not spending enough time with your partner are the last thing you want to happen.

It's just not what you want to give up all of these things. Being an MMA fighter comes with a price that you don't want to pay. If you turned this offer down, nobody would think you were crazy or a coward because most people recognize that the price is excessive.

I just gave an example, but it also applies to becoming a wealthy business owner. It is very expensive. A prosperous business owner can aspire to be as great as a boxer, writer, singer, or physician.

Most of us are aware that becoming a Medical Doctor requires years of rigorous study in order to become an average doctor, but we don't use the same reasoning to increase our income. It should be simple and quick. We anticipate no discomfort.

For instance, you wouldn't anticipate that a fat man with no prior boxing experience would prevail over an experienced boxer, but that is what most of us do when it comes to starting a business. The majority of us have neither started nor learned about starting a business in school.

The majority of us come from households with extremely low financial and business literacy. Though we resemble that overweight man, we anticipate striking first, trading blows, and eventually knocking outwit the more seasoned opponent.

This is the reason that most people launch a business, give up blaming others for their failures, and then the competitive landscape or the economy.

In actuality, they were unwilling to pay because they were unaware of the expense. Prior to beginning anything, ascertain its cost and whether you are genuinely ready to cover the cost of it.

Understanding the cost helped me to not give up very fast and be comfortable with slow progress.

Even though you are aware of the high cost of what you are doing, you persist after a few shortcomings.

When you weigh the costs, you realize that you must lead an unbalanced life, and pay that price by forgoing fun times, family, and friends.

Chapter 7: Become Wealthy At A Young Age This Image May Already Be Familiar To You.

An elderly couple was on a vacation. Sadly, they are so exhausted that they are unable to enjoy their boat tour "*hahaha*".

Please understand that I'm not mocking this couple; rather, I'm bringing them up because their photo has been a valuable reminder for me over the years.

This is what I mean.

I kept seeing this advice when I started reading books on investing and personal finance. If you invest even a tiny sum of money, like $5 per day, over time, you will possess more than $1 million in 40 years, which is accurate when it makes perfect sense, but I can still I always get this weird, contradictory feeling when I read advice like this.

I would first become ecstatic about the prospect of making a tiny investment and becoming wealthy.

However, I recall that after the fleeting thrill, I would become agitated. Yes, I will have a million dollars, but I will also be elderly, I would tell myself. When I'm in a wheelchair, do I still want to be wealthy? Do I want to take a vacation but am so tired that I just pass out?

I didn't want the million dollars when I was seventy-nine. I didn't want a fancy car when I was elderly and needed help getting around. Take a seat in that vehicle.

Eventually, one day, I stumbled upon MJ's book, The Millionaire Fastlane DeMarco, and it had a profound impact on my life.

This book explains how to start a business, invent something, and become wealthy quickly in order to retire early, or just making things that, in your youth, can make you a lot of money.

I understand that the phrase "Get Rich Quick" can seem deceptive, but the author discusses getting wealthy quickly does not imply becoming wealthy in a matter of weeks or months.

For instance, if you start a business, you may dedicate five or ten years to it, but after if you are successful, you won't ever have to work again. This is what he refers to as "Get Rich Quick," and when you compare it, ten years seems quick to make 40 years of investments.

While I always recommend this book because it's one of my favorites, there's one thing I don't find amusing that it sort of mocks long-term investing.

As I previously stated, starting a business has expenses, and not everyone is happy with their employment and don't want the burden of major responsibilities and stress.

For these individuals, investing $5 every day for 40 years at an average salary could be a wise choice. I personally engage in it as well, but I don't count on it to bring me fortune in the future. I suppose everything relies on your true desires.

Check out this book if you want to retire early and never work again in your life.

However, if your job and long-term investment are fulfilling, stick with them. Remember that compound interest works its magic at the conclusion of the term.

For instance, Warren Buffett's wealth was acquired after the age of fifty by ninety percent. While investing is Warren Buffett's forte, time is his secret. Since he was a young boy, he has been an investor.

Chapter 8: Think Big

During my time in college, I had a classmate who was constantly discussing the significance of being practical in daily life.

When he observed someone making a significant move or having lofty ambitions, he would remind them to return to the real world.

For instance, when a few of our classmates discussed studying in the United States. Come on, be realistic, he would quickly say there. You can't even introduce yourself in English, and you're broke. How are you going to learn in that place?

Not just with other people. That was how he was with himself, too. He'd say things like, "I know that I will never drive an expensive Mercedes," and my bank account is loaded with a million dollars.

Please understand that he wasn't a bad person at all. On the contrary, he was a kind and trustworthy friend. On difficult days, you could go to him as a friend to borrow money or his coat for a noteworthy occasion.

His narrow-mindedness was the only issue. He refused to even allow himself to have lofty dreams.

According to David Schwartz, the author of The Magic of Thinking Big, the big thinkers discover the possibilities and things they can accomplish in life, not only the current state of their life.

Conversely, small thinkers see nothing beyond what is directly in front of them. Otherwise, a narrow-minded person would say, "This is an old house in very bad condition," upon seeing its condition, resulting in a $50,000 sales price.

However, visionaries will view the same home and conclude that, indeed, this is an old house, but I can renovate, clean up the yard, and plant trees around the house and get $100,000 for its sale.

Put simply, one perceives reality, while another perceives possibilities. The majority of people are incapable of having big dreams or even big thoughts. I'm not saying that everything will be wonderful if you think big.

It's only the first step to think big; there are probably a hundred more to follow. Let's take an example where you are now earning $1,000 per month and you begin to set ambitious goals.

Thus, your primary objective is to earn $10,000 per month. Setting the goal and thinking big will help it start directing you toward your destination like a GPS.

You will soon begin to behave differently and in a different way. You're going to start reading different books, watching different videos, and turning down some friends. Big ideas will inspire big actions, and big actions will result in big things

You can't have the things that the big person has until you first become the big person you want to be and then follow in their footsteps. The majority of people think the opposite is true.

They claim that once I have $10,000 per month, I will begin to live as someone who makes $10,000 per month would.

I can only then transform into that person. It doesn't work like that. You have to become the person first and only then the rest will come.

And this can't happen if you don't allow yourself to think big. I have personally learned two important lessons about thinking big.

First of all, I discovered that a lot of big goals are simpler to accomplish than small ones because, when you set big goals, you come to terms with the fact that you cannot accomplish them alone. Thus, you must involve other people.

Utilizing the knowledge and experience of others makes things much simpler to accomplish.

Small goals, on the other hand, limit your thinking to what you can accomplish on your own.

Second, I became aware that my previously perceived lofty objectives weren't actually that lofty.

Furthermore, the issues I believed to be significant turned out not to be so.

Simply put, I was too small.

Chapter 9.

Life Energy Equals Money

Most of us think that our jobs support our lives, according to Vicky Robbins, author of the book Your Money or Your Life.

In actuality, though, our work becomes our life. The majority of us work far more than 40 hours a week in order to make a living.

For instance, we need to budget time for getting ready for work, making the commute, and thinking about our jobs both at work and at home. We have to lose ourselves in mindless entertainment on the weekends and in the evenings in order to decompress and unwind.

We plan almost every aspect of our lives around our jobs. We labor because we want to make money. This perspective makes it clear that you are selling your life for e energy is equal to money.
I became more conscious of my spending w hen I began to view money as my life force. I had to consider whether an item was worth my life energy each time I wanted to purcha se it.

I began to see prices expressed in weeks or h ours of my life rather than dollars or euros.

For instance, the new phone I wanted to buy was no longer $800, but instead required me to work at a job I didn't enjoy for one month .

And I am aware of your thoughts financial gain. Life energy is equal to money. I became more conscious of my spending when I began to view money as my life force. I had to consider whether an item was worth my life energy each time I wanted to purchase it.

I began to see prices expressed in weeks or hours of my life rather than dollars or euros. For instance, the new phone I wanted to buy was no longer $800, but instead required me to work at a job I didn't enjoy for one month. And I am aware of your thoughts. You're thinking that this is just forcing yourself to feel guilty about every purchase, so that you don't make that purchase, but that's not true.

When you see your money as your life energy, you suddenly value it more. And when you value it more, you start spending it on the things that you truly want, instead of spending it on a second pair of shoes that you'll probably wear only once.

Here's a question for you. What is the price of your life energy?

How much is your every hour truly worth?

The traditional way to calculate this is simply to take the amount of your net pay and divide it by the number of hours you have to work. For example, if you work 160 hours per month and your net monthly salary is $500, then we need to divide $500 by 160 and that equals $3 and 12.5 per hour.

However, it's not that simple. To calculate your real hourly wage, you need to take into account other factors, such as the time and money you use for everything related to your work.

Think of all the money you must spend to keep your jobs, such as transport costs, the costs of eating outside, the cost of living in an expensive city because that is where your job is, and medical costs because of work-related stress. You need to deduct all those job-related expenses. This is how you'll know what you earn for each hour of your life's energy.

Chapter 10: Create Your Own Fortune

I'm starting to doubt the value of luck in business as time goes on. The majority of the time, what people refer to as luck is simply the outcome of numerous actions. Let's take an example where you and I are trying to find an investment property to purchase. You check 100 flats, and I go check ten. Who do you believe will be fortunate?

Naturally, you will have more luck, but from the outside, it will appear as though you recently discovered and purchased a fantastic property. Your chances of hitting it lucky increase with the number of actions you take. Because they make their own luck, people who take action tend to be luckier.

I was inspired by this lesson to try a lot of different things and to be okay with the majority of them failing. I discovered that it is possible to be largely incorrect and still achieve great success. For instance, Warren Buffett acknowledged that over the course of his career, he has owned stock in more than 400 different companies. Only ten of them yielded the largest gains.

This reality is also understood by many large companies. For instance, only a small number of Netflix's produced series have achieved widespread success, if you look through the entire catalog. Once you understand this, you can accept that many things failing or going wrong is common.

Sometimes all it takes to transform your life is one concept, one book, one phrase, one person, or one video.

Viewers from the outside will assume that you simply got lucky and connected with the one person who made all the difference in your success. However, what they fail to realize is that you likely reached out to over 50 people before you found that one person.

Your own luck was made. This concludes our lesson; however, I have one more bonus lesson to wrap up everything we covered in this book. I mentioned at the beginning of the book that I started reading in order to make more money, but as I went along, I came to understand that reading has very little to do with money.

It's much more than that. For instance, you may quickly discover that your body and mind are deteriorating if you start working fifteen hours a day just to make more money. This is because you are spending all day sitting in your room.

After you begin regular exercise, you find that improving your diet and sleep patterns is also necessary. It is not possible to consistently consume junk food, stay up late, and work 15 hours a day. You may look around your room after returning from the gym and exclaim, "It's unbelievable that I live and work in such a mess!!"

Thus, you begin maintaining the room's cleanliness and order. You begin to feel better, but you are still unhappy and pessimistic for some reason. Now is the time to begin listening more intently to that constant voice in your head. Thus, you begin studying meditation and mastering the deranged roommate in your mind. You used to laugh at people who discussed spirituality and meditation, but these days you practice meditation yourself.

You gained self-control and emotional regulation skills. You used to get upset and furious at every little thing that someone said or did. You just let it go now, though. You pick up new behaviors and give up unhealthy ones, like smoking. You can stop hanging out with certain friends now that you don't smoke. You soon begin to walk and speak differently.

You quit dressing like an 11-year-old teenager and start sporting more fitted t-shirts and jeans. You begin dressing nicely because you recognize the significance of making a good first impression on potential business partners. As the years go by and you continue to get better, one day you look back and realize that you have reached your financial objective.

However, the individual positioned above the finish line has changed. You are no longer the same person—mentally or physically. You have experienced a total personal metamorphosis. At this point, you understand that your accomplishments are far more significant than your financial situation and have little to do with it.

Appreciation and Summary

For the time and effort you invested in reading this book, I would want to sincerely thank you. Your decision to peruse these pages and discover the truths they provide is incredibly admirable in a world full of infinite possibilities. There's something special about books that allows for reflection and personal development. I hope that you found resonance in the concepts discussed here, (The 10 Powerful Lessons That Made Me a Millionaire, 2024) and that they enhanced your own growth.

This book was strongly powered by Bernard k. s